N.Y. (State) PUBLIC SERVICE COMMISSION

FOR THE FIRST DISTRICT

STATE OF NEW YORK

Rules of Procedure and Regulations Governing Matters before the Commission

Adopted July 29, 1910

Effective Sept. 1, 1910

William R. Willcox, *Chairman*
William McCarroll
Edward M. Bassett
Milo R. Maltbie
John E. Eustis

Travis H. Whitney, *Secretary*,
154 Nassau Street, New York City.

L 1080

2500-Ag. 10-(LRC)

Rules of Procedure and Regulations Governing Matters before the Public Service Commission for the First District

Adopted July 29, 1910.

Effective Sept. 1, 1910.

RULE I. Sessions of the Commission.

Public sessions of the Commission will be held on Tuesday and Friday of each week, unless otherwise ordered.

RULE II. Secretary to Furnish Information.

The Secretary to the Commission will, upon request, advise as to the form of petition, answer, or other papers necessary to be filed in any case, and furnish such information from the files of the Commission as will conduce to a full presentation of material facts.

RULE III. General Matters Applicable to all Cases.

1. *Address of the Commission.* All papers and communications should be addressed to "Public Service Commission, 154 Nassau Street, Borough of Manhattan, New York City."

2. *Case Numbers and Titles.* Each matter coming formally before the Commission will be known as a case and shall receive a number and a title, descriptive of the subject matter. Such number and title shall be used on all papers in the case.

3. *Documents Filed* with the Commission shall be printed or typewritten, and, so far as practicable, shall be upon paper 8x11 inches in size.

4. *Service of Papers.* Notices or other papers may be served personally or by mail as provided by Section 23 of the Public Service Commissions Law and by the Code of Civil Procedure, and when any party has appeared by attorney, service upon such attorney will be deemed proper service upon the party.

5. *Witnesses and Subpoenas.* Subpoenas requiring the attendance of witnesses for the purpose of taking testimony may, upon the application of any party, be signed and issued by any member of the Commission or by the Secretary.

Subpoenas for the production of books, papers or documents (unless directed to issue by the Commission upon its own motion) will only be issued, in the discretion of a Commissioner, upon application in writing.

6. *Amendments.* The Commission may, in its discretion, allow any complaint, answer, petition or other paper to be amended or corrected or omission to be supplied therein.

7. *Orders.* All orders made by the Commission will be filed in the office of the Commission and certified copies thereof shall be served upon the parties to be affected thereby.

RULE IV. Hearings and Rehearings.

1. *When Hearing Will Be Given.* Except as determined otherwise in specific cases, the Commission will grant or fix a hearing in the following classes of cases:

(a) Where an order to satisfy a complaint or to make answer thereto has been made and the person or corporation complained against has not satisfied the cause of the complaint. (See Rule V.)

(b) Where a complaint against a gas or electric company has been made, as prescribed by Rule VI.

(c) Where application has been made for the approval, determination, consent, permission, certificate or authorization of the Commission, or for extension of time in which to file a periodic report. (See Rules VII-XVI.)

2. *Notice of Hearing.*

(a) Notice of the day and hour of a hearing shall be served upon all interested parties at least ten days before the date of hearing, unless the Commission prescribes a shorter notice. (For form see Rule XX [3].)

(b) Hearings, unless otherwise directed by the Commission, will be at the office of the Commission, in a room assigned by the Secretary.

3. *Procedure at Hearings and Rehearings.* At a hearing witnesses will be examined orally unless otherwise ordered by the Commissioner, or unless with the consent of the Commissioner the facts are agreed upon. Parties will be afforded all reasonable opportunity for presenting evidence and examining and cross-examining witnesses.

The complainant may establish the facts alleged, unless the same are admitted in the answer, or the Commission may investigate the facts relevant to the issue or the subject matter complained of. The person or corporation complained against must fully disclose its defense at the hearing, but in case of failure to answer, the Commission will take such proof of the facts and make such order thereon as the case requires.

4. *Adjournments.* Hearings may be adjourned from time to time by or at the direction of the Commission or any Commissioner.

5. *Briefs.* The Commission or any Commissioner will receive or may require the submission of briefs.

6. *Rehearings.* Applications for reopening a case after final submission, or for a rehearing after decision made by the Commis-

sion, must be in writing and must state specifically the grounds upon which the application is based, and fully the facts in support thereof. When any decision, order or requirement of the Commission is sought to be reversed, abrogated, changed or modified on account of facts and circumstances arising subsequent to the hearing or of consequences resulting from compliance with such decision, order or requirement which are claimed to justify a reconsideration of the case, the matters relied upon by the applicant must be fully set forth.

RULE V. Complaints as to Common Carriers under Section 48 of the Act.

1. *Contents of a Complaint.* A complaint must be by petition or complaint in writing, filed in duplicate, setting forth the facts claimed to constitute the thing or act done or omitted to be done in violation (1) of any provision of law or (2) of the terms and conditions of the franchise or charter of the company complained of or (3) of an order of the Commission. The petition or complaint must also contain allegations tending to show that the complainant is aggrieved by the acts or omissions complained of. The name of the person or corporation complained of should be stated in full and the address of the complainant, with the name and the address of his attorney or counsel, if any, must appear on the petition or complaint. (For form of such complaint see Rule XX [1].)

(a) Complaints regarding rates and charges shall not be joined with other complaints, nor shall wholly unrelated complaints be joined, nor except in the case of complaints regarding joint rates or through service shall two or more corporations be joined as defendants in one complaint without the consent of the Commission.

(b) No oral or unsigned complaint will be entertained or acted upon by the Commission.

(c) Where a complaint is submitted which is not in the form prescribed by this rule the Secretary may notify the party against whom the complaint is made of such complaint in order that the cause for complaint may be remedied without the necessity of the Commission taking formal action regarding same.

2. *Order upon Complaint.* The Commission may adopt an order, as to a complaint filed as herein prescribed, directed to the

person or corporation complained against, directing that the matters complained of be satisfied or that the charges be answered in writing within ten days from the date of such order, but the Commission may, in a particular case, require the answer to be filed within a shorter time. (For form of such order see Rule XX [2].)

3. *Answer to Complaint.*

(a) The original answer must be filed with the Secretary of the Commission at its office, and a copy thereof at the same time served, personally or by mail, upon the complainant, who must forthwith notify the Secretary of its receipt. Notice of the service of such copy must be filed with the Secretary of the Commission by the person or corporation complained of.

(b) The answer must specifically admit or deny the material allegations of the petition or complaint and set forth the facts which will be relied upon as a defense.

(c) If the person or corporation complained of satisfies the matters or charges contained in the complaint, in whole or in part, a written statement shall be filed by the defendant with the Secretary of the Commission, showing the extent of the satisfaction accorded.

4. *Hearing upon Complaint.* Upon issue being joined or upon failure of defendants to answer or make satisfaction, the Commission may fix a date for a hearing. (See Rule IV and for form of notice of hearing see Rule XX [3].)

RULE VI. Complaints as to Gas and Electric Companies under Section 71 of the Act.

The form and contents of complaints made as provided in Section 71 shall be as follows:

(1) The complaint shall be directed to the Public Service Commission for the First District. It shall state the names of the corporations supplying gas or electricity for heat, light or power, either within the City of New York or within such subdivision thereof, either county, borough or ward, as the complainants may desire to include within the complaint.

(2) If the complaint be against gas companies, it shall state whether it is directed to (a) the illuminating power or (b) purity or (c) the pressure or (d) the price of gas; if against electrical companies, whether directed to (a) the efficiency of the electric

incandescent lamp supply, or (b) the voltage of the current supplied for light, heat or power, or (c) the price of electricity sold and delivered. It shall specify the respects wherein the service is otherwise inadequate or the methods unreasonable, and if it is claimed that the price is excessive, unfair or unreasonable, the price actually charged by such companies should be set forth.

(3) The complaint, when made by customers or purchasers, shall state that each of the complainants is a customer or purchaser of either gas or electricity, as the case may be, from one or more of the said companies against whom the complaint is made.

(4) If the complaint relates to the price of either gas or electricity, it should state that the price is excessive, unjust or unreasonable and is disproportionate to the proper cost of manufacturing and delivering such gas or electricity in the locality mentioned.

(5) The complaint may also contain any other specifications of any illegal act on the part of said companies, or any violation of the charter or franchises of said companies or any of them, in respect of the manufacture, distribution, transmission or supply of gas or electricity, or in its methods of conducting its business, and should demand the relief which the complainant desires.

(6) The complaint must be signed by the Mayor or by not less than one hundred customers or purchasers or by an officer of a gas or electrical corporation in the City of New York, or in such lesser territory as is included in the complaint. Each complainant must add to his signature his place of residence, by street and number, if any.

(7) A single complaint shall not include both gas and electricity.

(8) Upon such complaint being filed an order for a hearing will be made returnable at such time as the Commission may direct. Such order may also include such other matters as the Commission may desire to include in the investigation or hearing. A certified copy of the order with a copy of the complaint shall be served on each corporation affected thereby, and the hearing shall proceed at the time and place designated or at such other time and place to which the Commission or the Commissioner presiding may adjourn the same. (See also Rule IV.)

RULE VII. General Rules as to Application to the Commission by Companies.

1. All applications for the approval, determination, consent, permission, certificate or authorization of the Commission in cases where such approval, determination, consent, permission, certificate

or authorization is required by law, shall be by petition, duly verified. Five copies of the petition shall also be filed. In all cases there must be annexed to the original petition certified or verified copies of the certificate of organization of every corporation directly affected by the proposed action, and certified copies of all such certificates, statements or records which modify, change or extend the purposes or powers of such corporations. When documents have already been filed with the Commission, the petitioner may, in lieu of filing additional copies, state in the petition such fact with the date of filing.

The petition must contain such further statements as are required by special provisions of law or by special rules governing the particular application and must show in detail compliance with all provisions of law as to such petition.

2. Upon the receipt of a petition required by this rule the same will be referred for examination. If it is found not to be correct in form, the Secretary will advise the applicant of the defects, who may correct the same. If the petition be found correct in form, the Commission will thereupon either make an order *ex parte* granting the application or will appoint a time and place for a public hearing. (See Rule IV.)

3. Where a hearing has been appointed the applicant may be required to publish in such papers and at such time as may be designated a notice of hearing to be known as "published notice of hearing" substantially in the form shown in Rule XX (5), and submitted for the approval of the Secretary to the Commission.

At or before the hearing the applicant must file with the Secretary to the Commission proof of due publication of such notice.

RULE VIII. Financial Condition Defined.

Wherever an applicant is required to set forth its financial condition, such financial condition shall be given so far as practicable in proper schedules annexed to and referred to and properly designated in the petition. Such schedules shall show the following:

(1) Amount and kinds of stock authorized.

(2) Amount and kinds of stock issued and outstanding.

(3) Terms of preference of all preferred stock.

(4) Brief description of each mortgage upon property of the applicant giving date of execution, name of mortgagor, name of mortgagee or trustee, amount of indebtedness authorized to be secured thereby and amount of indebtedness actually secured.

(5) Number and amount of bonds authorized and issued, giving name of company which issued and describing each class separately, giving date of issue, par value, rate of interest, date of maturity and how secured.

(6) Other indebtedness giving same by classes and describing security, if any. A brief statement showing devolution or assumption of any of the foregoing debts upon or by any person or corporation, if the original liability has been transferred.

(7) Amount of interest paid during previous fiscal year and rate thereof. If different rates were paid, amount paid at each rate.

(8) Rate and amount of dividends paid during previous five years.

(9) Detailed statement of earnings and expenditures for and balance sheet showing conditions at the close of last fiscal year, unless already filed with the Commission as part of the annual report.

RULE IX. Application for Certificate of Public Convenience and a Necessity under Section 9 of the Railroad Law.

When application is made for a certificate of public convenience and a necessity

1. The petition in addition to the requirements of Rule VII, must state:

(a) That a copy of the certificate of incorporation of the applicant has been published as required by Section 9 of the Railroad Law.

(b) That application is made within six months after the completion of such publication.

(c) The proposed route or routes, the method of construction and the motive power proposed to be employed on the route and the names of all railroads and street railroads with which the proposed road is likely to compete.

(d) The facts showing the proposed construction to be required by public convenience and necessity.

(e) The manner in which it is proposed to finance the proposed construction.

2. With the petition shall be filed:

(a) Proof of publication of the certificate of incorporation as required by Section 9 of the Railroad Law.

(b) Map showing the streets, avenues and all other places and property in which the road is to be constructed.

(c) Proof of payment of the organization tax by receipt of the State Treasurer.

3. Notice of hearing in the form prescribed in Rule XX (3) shall be served by the applicant, if required by the Commission, upon railroad corporations and street railroad corporations with which the proposed construction is likely to compete at least five days before the hearing and at or before the hearing proofs of the service of such notices shall be filed with the Secretary.

RULE X. Application for Permission and Approval of the Commission under Section 53 of the Public Service Commissions Law to the Construction and Operation of Extensions of Street Surface Railroads.

1. When application is made for the permission and approval to the construction and operation of extensions of a street railroad, in addition to the matters required by Rule VII, the petition shall:

(a) State the route of the proposed extension and the name of each railroad and street railroad corporation with which the proposed construction is likely to compete.

(b) State the facts showing that such construction and operation is necessary or convenient for the public service.

(c) State the manner in which it is proposed to finance the construction of the extension and give the financial condition of the applicant as defined in Rule VIII.

(d) State the motive power proposed to be employed on the route, and describe the method of construction on the proposed route.

2. With the petition there shall be filed:

(a) A certified copy of the certificate of Extension of Route filed in the office of the Secretary of State with the date of the filing thereof.

(b) A certified copy of the written application for the consent of the local authorities to the construction and operation of such extension, and the consent of the local authorities granted thereon.

(c) An affidavit of an officer of the company stating whether the consent of the abutting property owners has been obtained and recorded and if recorded the time and place of record, or a certified copy of the report of the Commission appointed by the Appellate Division of the Supreme Court pursuant to Section 174 of the Railroad Law and the order of the Court thereon, if such report and order have been made, and if such consent or report and order have not been obtained or made the petition shall contain a statement to that effect.

(d) A map of the said extension as proposed showing the streets, avenues and all other places and property in or upon which it is proposed to construct such extension.

3. The published notice of application and of hearing shall set forth the names and descriptions of the streets, roads, places and property upon which it is proposed to construct and operate such extension.

4. At the hearing proof must be made that the construction and operation of such extension are necessary or convenient for the public service, and proof must be made of the *bona fides* of the enterprise and of the financial ability of the applicant to build the extension.

RULE XI. Application for the Permission and Approval of the Commission under Section 53 or 68 of the Act Except in a Case Covered by Rule X.

When application is made for permission and approval under Section 53 or 68 of the Public Service Commissions Law, except as governed by Rule X,

1. The petition in addition to the requirements of Rule VII, shall state:

(a) The facts showing compliance with all provisions of law respecting the organization of the applicant and its right to begin construction or exercise the franchise or right for which permission and approval are sought, and a reference to each and every document filed with the Commission affecting the same.

(b) The financial condition of the applicant as defined in Rule VIII and the proposed method of financing the proposed construction or operation.

(c) If consents of property owners are required to be

obtained, whether such consents have been obtained and recorded and if recorded the time and place of record, or a certified copy of the report of the Commission appointed by the Appellate Division of the Supreme Court pursuant to Section 174 of the Railroad Law and the order of the Court thereon, if any.

(d) Whether the applicant, if a railroad corporation or street railroad corporation, has prior to June 6, 1907, received any certificate of public convenience and a necessity for any purpose and if so, a certified copy of the same should be annexed.

(e) If the application is for permission to exercise a franchise or right not theretofore lawfully exercised, the reason why such franchise or right has not been theretofore exercised.

(f) The facts showing that the construction or the exercise of the franchise or privilege for which the permission and approval of the Commission are sought is necessary or convenient for the public service.

2. With the petition shall be filed all documents, so far as pertinent to the application, enumerated in Rule X, Subdivision 2, a, b, c, d.

3. At the hearing proof must be made by the applicant of full compliance with all provisions of law respecting the organization of the applicant and its right to begin the construction or extension proposed or to exercise the franchise or privilege for which the permission and approval of the Commission are sought; and that such construction or the exercise of such franchise or right is necessary or convenient for the public service; and in all cases proof must be made of the *bona fides* of the enterprise and of the financial ability of the applicant to make the construction or to operate or use the franchise or right in such a way as to benefit the public service.

RULE XII. Application under Section 54 or 70 of the Act for Approval of Assignment, Transfer or Lease of Franchise, Works or System.

When application is made for approval by the Commission of an assignment, transfer or lease of the franchise, works or system of an applicant;

1. The petition must be made by all of the parties to the proposed transaction and in addition to the requirements of Rule VII must state:

(a) The financial condition of each applicant as defined in Rule VIII.

(b) In detail the reasons upon the part of each applicant for making the proposed assignment, transfer, lease, contract or agreement and all the facts warranting the same and showing that it is for the benefit of the public service.

2. There must be annexed to the petition copies of the proposed assignment, contract, lease or agreement, and if any prior agreements have been made between the parties relating to the same subject matter copies of such agreements must be annexed to the petition or referred to therein as already on file with the Commission.

RULE XIII. Application under Section 54 or 70 of the Act for Authorization to Purchase or Acquire Stock.

When an application is made for authorization to purchase or acquire the stock of a corporation,

1. The petition must be made by the corporation proposing to acquire the stock and, in addition to the requirements of Rule VII, must set forth:

(a) The financial condition of the applicant and of the corporation whose stock is sought to be acquired or held, as defined in Rule VIII.

(b) The reasons why the applicant desires to make the purchase and the amount of such stock already owned or held by applicant.

(c) Price proposed to be paid for the stock, the names of the present owners and the terms of payment with the market value thereof, with highest and lowest price during the period of at least one year prior to the application, and dividends, if any, paid for a period of five years.

RULE XIV. Application under Section 55 or 69 of the Act for Approval to the Issuance of Securites.

When application is made for the consent of the Commission to the issuance of securities,

1. The petition, in addition to the requirements of Rule VII, shall set forth:

(a) The financial condition of the applicant as defined in Rule VIII, and a description of the road, plant or system and equipment of the applicant, and a statement of the cost of existing property and of the amount of any of its stock held by other corporations and their names, and the kinds of stock held by each.

(b) A statement of the amount and kind of stock which the corporation desires to issue, and, if preferred, the nature and extent of the preference, a statement of the amount of bonds, notes, and other evidences of indebtedness which the corporation desires to issue, the terms, the rate of interest and whether and how to be secured, and if to be secured by a mortgage or pledge, the terms thereof.

(c) A statement of the use to which the capital to be secured by the issue of such stock, bonds, notes or other evidence of indebtedness is to be put, with a definite statement of how much is to be used severally for the acquisition of property, the construction, completion, extension or improvement of facilities, the improvement of its service, the maintenance of its service, the discharge or refunding of its obligations, and the reimbursement of moneys actually expended from income or from any other moneys in the treasury as provided by Sections 55 and 69.

(d) A statement in detail of the property which is to be acquired with its value, a detailed description of the construction, completion, extension or improvement of facilities set forth in such a manner that an estimate may be made of its cost, a statement of the character of the improvement of its service proposed, and of the reasons why the service should be maintained from its capital; if it is proposed to discharge or refund its obligations or to reimburse moneys actually expended, a statement of the nature and description of such obligations and expenditures, including the par value of the obligations and the amount for which they were actually sold and the application of the proceeds and of the moneys expended, showing when, to whom and for what paid or applied.

(e) A statement showing whether any contracts have been made for the acquisition of such property, or for such construction, completion, extension or improvement of facilities, or for the reimbursement of expenditures, or for the disposition of any of the stock, bonds, notes or evidence of indebtedness which it is proposed to issue or the avails thereof, and if any such contracts have been made, copies thereof should be annexed to the petition.

(f) A statement showing whether any of the outstanding stock or bonds or other obligations of the company have been issued or used in capitalizing any franchise or any right to own, operate or enjoy any franchise or any contract for consolidation or lease, and if so, the amount thereof and the franchise, right, contract or lease so capitalized.

(g) If the stock is to be issued by a corporation formed by the merger or consolidation of two or more other corporations, the petition shall contain a complete statement of the financial condition of the corporations so to be merged or consolidated of the kind required by subdivision (a) hereinabove set forth, and of their capital stock at the par value thereof.

(h) The petition shall contain a statement of other facts pertinent to the application.

2. With the petition shall be filed:

(a) If application is in regard to an increase or reduction of capital stock, a certificate of the proceedings at the meeting of stockholders or unanimous consent of the stockholders as required by the Stock Corporations Law.

(b) If the application is in regard to a mortgage, proof of the consent of the stockholders under the Stock Corporations Law and the Railroad Law.

3. The order granting an application will:

(a) Prescribe the purposes for which securities or obligations authorized or the proceeds thereof shall be used.

(b) Direct the applicant to report under oath the sale or sales of the securities or obligations authorized, the terms and conditions of sale and the amounts realized therefrom.

(c) Require the applicant to make a verified report at least every six months showing in detail the use and application by it of the moneys so realized until such moneys shall have been fully expended.

RULE XV. Application for Consent to Discontinue a Station.

On an application for the consent of the Commission to discontinue a station,

1. The petition shall, in addition to the matters required by Rule VII, state:

(a) The facts upon which the applicant relies for the consent.

(b) Whether the station is situated on a line operated under lease or other agreement.

(c) Whether there is any agreement with the lessor or predecessor as to the maintenance of the station.

(d) Whether there is any agreement between the applicant or its lessor or predecessor and any person or persons, association or corporation or municipality, with reference to the maintenance of the station at the point in question.

(e) Whether any application as to the station in question has heretofore been made to the Board of Railroad Commissioners or to the Public Service Commission for the First District.

2. With the petition should be filed certified copies of any such agreements as are not already on file with the Commission.

RULE XVI. Application for Extension of Time to File Annual or Periodic Reports or Comply with an Order of the Commission.

When an application is made for extension of time within which to make and file any annual or periodic report with the Commission or to comply with an order of the Commission,

1. The petition, filed before the expiration of the period prescribed, shall be set forth in detail:

(a) What, if any, effort has been made by the applicant to prepare such report or to comply with the order:

(b) Any facts tending to show why the said report cannot be made and filed or the order complied with within the time prescribed;

(c) Any other facts which may make an extension of time necessary or proper;

(d) The further period of time deemed necessary by the applicant within which to make and file such report or to comply with the order.

2. The Commission may direct a hearing upon said petition and in that event the applicant shall attend before the Commissioner presiding and produce such witnesses and documents in the matter as the Commission shall require.

RULE XX. Forms Prescribed for Use.

Forms of papers shall be substantially as follows:

1. Form of Complaint against Railroad or Street Railroad Companies or Other Common Carriers.

To the Public Service Commission for the First District:

The complaint (or petition) of (name and address of complainant) respectfully shows:

That (here state the name of person or corporation complained of) (and set forth the facts which complainant claims constitute a cause of complaint, with a statement showing how the complainant is aggrieved thereby).

2. Wherefore complainant asks (here state the relief to which complainant believes he is entitled).

(Date.)

....

Complainant's name and address.

....

Name and address of attorney, if any.

2. Form of Order to Satisfy or Answer a Complaint.

TITLE. SEE RULE III (2).	CASE NO...................... COMPLAINT ORDER.

The complaint herein having been received and filed:

Ordered: That the matter therein complained of be satisfied or that the charges be answered in writing by the said company within ten days from the service upon it of a certified copy of this order and of a copy of the complaint.

3. Form of Notice of a Hearing.

TITLE. SEE RULE III (2).	CASE NO....................... NOTICE OF HEARING.

Please Take Notice that the Public Service Commission for the First District will give a hearing in the above entitled matter on (day of week) (day of month) at o'clock M., at the offices of the Commission, at No. 154 Nassau Street, Borough of Manhattan, City of New York, or at such other time and place to which the same may be adjourned.

By the Commission,

....

Secretary.

To ....

4. Form of Acknowledgment by a Company of Receipt of an Order of the Commission, as Required by Section 23 of the Public Service Commissions Law.

TITLE. SEE RULE III (2).	CASE NO....................... ACKNOWLEDGMENT OF RECEIPT OF ORDER.

PUBLIC SERVICE COMMISSION:

You are hereby notified that a certified copy of an order in the above entitled matter adopted by the Public Service Commission for the First District on (date) was received by the Company on the day of , 19 .

Dated, , 19 .

(Signed) ....

Name and title of officer as required by Section 23.

CITY OF NEW YORK, }
County of } ss.:

On this day of , 19 , before me personally came , to me known, and known to me to be the (title of officer) of the Company and the person who signed the foregoing notice, and he duly acknowledged to me that he signed the same.

....

Commissioner of Deeds
or
Notary Public.

5. Form of Published Notice of Hearing (See Rule VII [2])

TITLE. SEE RULE III (2).	CASE NO.................. PUBLISHED NOTICE OF HEARING.

NOTICE is hereby given that the application of (name of applicant in full) for the (approval, determination, consent, permission, certificate, or authorization) of the Public Service Commission for the First District to (here state the nature of the consent asked for) will be heard by said Commission at its office, 154 Nassau Street, Borough of Manhattan, New York City, on the day of at o'clock in the noon.

Dated .

(Name of applicant.)

STATE OF NEW YORK
PUBLIC SERVICE COMMISSION
FOR THE FIRST DISTRICT

RULE XXVII OF THE RULES OF PROCEDURE OF THE PUBLIC SERVICE COMMISSION FOR THE FIRST DISTRICT, ADOPTED MAY 4, 1909.

Governing Applications under Section 34 of the Railroad Law for the Consent of the Commission to the Discontinuance of a Station or Stations.

RULE XXVII.

1. The application for such consent shall be by petition verified by the president or other officer of the railroad company.

2. The petition shall set forth at length the facts upon which the petition is based and the reasons why, in the opinion of the petitioner, the station or stations mentioned in the petition should be discontinued and shall ask that the consent of the Commission to the discontinuance thereof be granted.

3. The petition shall state whether the station or stations sought to be discontinued are situated on a line operated by the petitioner under a lease or other agreement. A copy of any such lease or agreement shall accompany the petition and shall be filed therewith.

4. The petition shall state whether there is any agreement of any kind between the company and its lessor or predecessor with reference to the maintenance of stations. A copy of any such agreement shall accompany the petition and shall be filed therewith.

5. The petition shall state whether there is any agreement of any kind between the company or its lessor or predecessor and any person or persons, association, corporation or municipality with reference to the maintenance of a station or stations at the point or points mentioned in the petition. Copies of all such agreements shall accompany the petition and shall be filed therewith.

6. If any of the documents hereinabove required have been already filed with the Commission duplicates need not be filed but the petition shall show that they have already been filed and the date of filing.

7. The petition shall show whether any previous application has been made to the Board of Railroad Commissioners or to the Public Service Commission for the First District for the consent of the Board of Railroad Commissioners or of the Public Service Commission for the First District to the discontinuance of the station or stations mentioned in the petition and shall give the date of any such application and shall state what action was taken thereon.

8. Upon receipt of such petition the Commission shall appoint a time and place for a hearing upon such application, giving to the petitioner at least ten days' notice thereof, either personally or by mail, and the petitioner shall publish a notice of such application and of the time and place of said hearing in such newspapers and at such times as the Commission shall prescribe and shall file proof of said publication with the Secretary of the Public Service Commission for the First District on or before the opening of said hearing; and said petitioner shall post copies of said notice in the station or stations sought to be discontinued and at such other places as the Commission may by order direct in such manner and at such time as the Commission may by its order direct and shall file proof of the posting of said notices with the Secretary of the Public Service Commission for the First District on or before the opening of said hearing.

www.ingramcontent.com/pod-product-compliance
Lightning Source LLC
LaVergne TN
LVHW020633110826
845149LV00004B/1163

* 9 7 8 1 4 1 8 1 8 6 6 4 7 *